Pathfinder 22

A CILT series for language teachers

Developing skills for independent reading

Iain Mitchell and Ann Swarbrick

CiLT

Other titles in the PATHFINDER series:

Reading for pleasure in a foreign language (Ann Swarbrick)
Communication re-activated: teaching pupils with learning difficulties
 (Bernardette Holmes)
Yes - but will they behave? Managing the interactive classroom
 (Susan Halliwell)
On target - teaching in the target language (Susan Halliwell and Barry Jones)
Bridging the gap: GCSE to 'A' level (John Thorogood and Lid King)
Making the case for languages (Alan Moys and Richard Townsend)
Languages home and away (Alison Taylor)
Being creative (Barry Jones)
Departmental planning and schemes of work (Clive Hurren)
Progressing through the Attainment Targets (Ian Lane)
Continuous assessment and recording (John Thorogood)
Fair enough? Equal opportunities and modern languages (Vee Harris)
Improve your image: the effective use of the OHP
 (Daniel Tierney and Fay Humphreys)
Not bothered? Motivating reluctant learners in Key Stage 4
 (Jenifer Alison)
Grammar matters (Susan Halliwell)
Differentiation (Anne Convery and Do Coyle)
Drama in the languages classroom (Judith Hamilton and Anne McLeod)
Nightshift - ideas and strategies for homework
 (David Buckland and Mike Short)
Creative use of texts (Bernard Kavanagh and Lynne Upton)

First published 1994
Copyright © 1994 Centre for Information on Language Teaching and Research
ISBN 1 874016 34 8

Cover by Logos Design & Advertising
Printed in Great Britain by Oakdale Printing Co Ltd

Published by the Centre for Information on Language Teaching and Research,
20 Bedfordbury, Covent Garden, London WC2N 4LB.

All rights reserved. No part of this publication may be reproduced, stored in a retrieval system, or transmitted in any form or by any means, electronic, mechanical, photocopying, recording, or otherwise, without the prior permission of the Copyright owner.

Contents

	Page
Introduction	1
What may we assume about our pupils?	1
What should we not assume?	3
1. Strategies for reading	4
Starting with the pupils	4
Reading the whole text	8
Some approaches to whole texts	
2. Making the most of available texts	11
Getting started - giving pupils confidence	11
Initial skimming	
Choosing what to look for, and how	
Keeping in the target language	
Doing a bit extra	
More intensive work	
Texts are not answers to questions	14
Headlines	
True or false?	
An extension task	
Using longer texts	16
Whole class warm-up activities	
Intensive reading	
A generic method	
Developing narrative awareness	20
Writing before reading	
Organising the story line	
Exploiting pre-knowledge	
No pre-knowledge	
Why was a text written?	28
3. Developing a policy for independent reading	30
Setting up an independent reading scheme	31
The Grange School, Avon	
Cottenham Village College, Cambridgeshire	
Reading diaries	36
The diary as a dialogue	
Conclusion	39
References	40

Introduction

The place of reading in the MFL curriculum has long been a subject of debate. With the emergence of the communicative approach many considered it to have lost its place to oral and aural activities. But educational trends have a way of coming into and going out of fashion. The importance of reading is no exception. There is now growing interest in schools in finding ways of activating pupils' interest in reading in another language. This book discusses ways in which departments might develop pupils' skills through a planned programme of reading including reading for pleasure.

The first Pathfinder on reading (Swarbrick, 1991) discussed a reading scheme developed to encourage pupils to read more widely in a foreign language. This Pathfinder seeks to extend that work to suggest that though it is important for learners to be offered a wide range of texts and to be given opportunities to read them, simply providing texts and opportunities for reading does not answer all of the needs of pupils. If pupils are to read the foreign language successfully, they need to be taught how to do so.

We shall set to our task beginning with the assumptions we make about the skills our pupils have when we meet them as beginning linguists (Introduction). We then discuss the strategies pupils might usefully develop to equip them to function independently when they meet unfamiliar texts (Section 1). We also suggest how teachers might develop these systematically using examples of readily available texts from textbooks (Section 2). We finish by focusing on reading for pleasure providing examples of work in practice from a variety of schools where developing a reading policy is considered a priority (Section 3).

WHAT MAY WE ASSUME ABOUT OUR PUPILS?

The prospect of learning a foreign language for many pupils is an exciting one. In the most successful classrooms pupils in their eagerness to speak the language quickly begin to use strategies in the spoken language which they use in their own language. They are not inexperienced communicators; they have a knowledge, from using their own language, of many communicative strategies. This is also true of their background as readers. They are not learning to read from scratch, they are learning to read in another language. There is an important difference. Most pupils, when they begin learning a language in their early teens or in the later years of primary school, have an implicit knowledge of what it is to read. For instance, many understand the significance of genre, they are, in general, able to recognise, say, journalistic register. They have a knowledge of print convention and of layout within different texts; for example, they could differentiate between a children's story and a travel brochure. They have a knowledge of the culture in which they live and this may inform their reading on certain topics. They have an awareness of how a story is formed; that it has a beginning, a middle and an end. They have a knowledge of punctuation. They will often be able to analyse the text in terms of the techniques being used to encourage the reader to read on, for example, in advertising brochures.

Though pupils come as experienced readers of their own language, much of this knowledge will be implicit. The challenge to the language teacher is to make what is implicit explicit. We cannot assume that all of these skills are transferred by pupils automatically. Faced with a text in a foreign language there may well be, for example, an initial panic reaction of incomprehension where many of the clues they would normally pick up from the text are ignored. This is well illustrated in a report on an INSET session run by Marion Giles Jones during which she describes the reactions of language teachers when faced with a Romanian text. Her aim was to encourage teachers to come to an understanding of the feelings of their pupils by presenting them with a text in a language unknown to them. Their reactions proved remarkably similar to the reactions of pupils.

> *The initial reaction was panic. Frustration due to feelings of inadequacy was common, and, surprisingly, in the case of one person, a feeling of total failure and a wish to give up trying almost immediately. Frustration was seen as positive by those who felt the challenge of the occasion; pleasure was expressed, and surprise on discovering how much was possible with minimum help. The value of previous knowledge was realised, the importance of clues such as layout, the timing of the help before despair sets in, and the importance of discussion.*
> (Giles Jones, 1988)

It is, then, useful to have an understanding of what reading skills pupils have developed in general terms before they begin learning the new language. If we do not take prior knowledge into consideration we are in danger of assuming that pupils have learnt nothing from their previous experience and down this track lies demotivation and under-achievement. A discussion with primary colleagues from feeder schools could prove invaluable to you.

WHAT SHOULD WE NOT ASSUME?

There is a fine line to be drawn between what we can assume many pupils know and reality. Though pupils may be able to judge the genre of a text by, for example, considering print convention, there are basic skills which we should not necessarily assume all pupils have. For instance, some pupils may not have a knowledge of alphabetical order, they may not have an awareness that in reading for different purposes the reading process changes; for instance, faced with a page of classified ads the skilled reader will scan the page for the information they are looking for rather than read every word. Pupils may not be interested in reading, in which case it becomes the teacher's task to convince the class that there is something in it for them. These issues may well have to be tackled at the outset if pupils are to become confident readers of the foreign language.

In other words, our task is greater than providing texts for pupils. We need to teach them reading strategies in order for them to gain independence as linguists. What these strategies are and how we teach them is the subject of the next section.

1. Strategies for reading

STARTING WITH THE PUPILS

What strategies do pupils themselves perceive they use when reading in a foreign language? We gave pupils who had been studying German for a year in a class of mixed attainment the following text and asked them, with a partner, to underline all the words they understood.

Liz, 19 Jahre, Irland

Das Mädchen mit dem Stirnband kommt aus Dublin, der Hauptstadt Irlands. Seit einem Jahr studiert sie in Limerick Wirtschaft und Deutsch. Liz lebt mit 7 Leuten zusammen in einem Haus. Ihr Berufswunsch ist Wirtschaftsprüferin. Sie ist schon in vielen Ländern Europas gewesen, denn Reisen ist ihr größtes Hobby. Frankreich, die Schweiz, Spanien, Italien, die Niederlande, Belgien, England und Deutschland hat sie besucht. Drei Städte haben Liz besonders beeindruckt: Frankfurt 'wegen der Atmosphäre', Berlin 'wegen der Geschichte' und Paris, 'wegen der Gebäude'. Deutsch ist ihr Lieblingsfach, darum nutzt sie die Semesterferien, um die Sprache zu lernen. Im nächsten Jahr will sie sechs Monate in die Bundesrepublik kommen. Sie muß in einem deutschen Büro ein Praktikum für ihr Studium machen.

'In unserem Land gibt es viele Arbeitslose', berichtet Liz. Darum kann sie sich gut vorstellen, in einem Land wie Deutschland zu arbeiten. Europa ist nützlich, wenn man beruflich etwas erreichen will, denkt Liz. Das Leben findet sie in Frankreich am interessantesten, denn 'dort ist es schön, und die Leute sind nett.'

Taken from a Juma magazine

The results were then pooled and somewhat to their surprise they realised that as a group they understood most of the words in the text. (Though this does beg the question of whether they understood the text as a whole as opposed to the individual words.) We asked them to reflect on how they had worked out the meaning of lexical items. Here are some of the strategies they were able to identify:

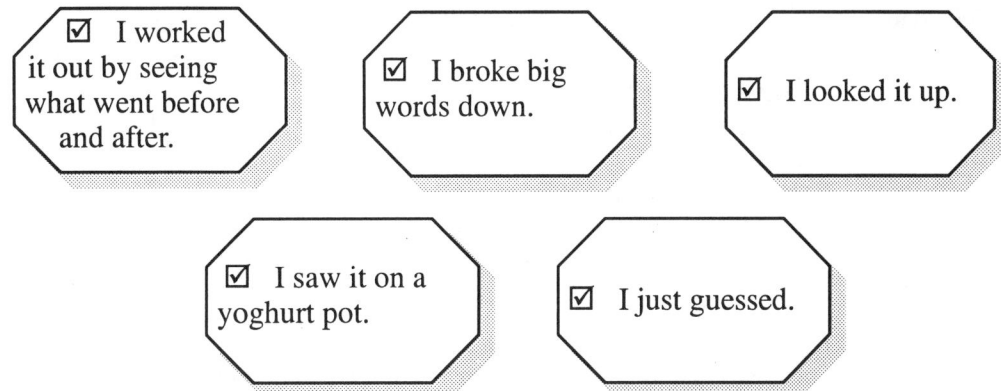

Not all pupils were using the same strategies and indeed there were some possibilities that none of them had considered but it highlights the fact that learners do bring some knowledge of how to approach unfamiliar text. As we mentioned earlier, their experience of reading in their first language has equipped them with some strategies. In other words, they do not come cold to the task of reading. The teacher's role, however, must be to extend the range for all pupils by explicitly teaching reading strategies.

Let's begin with a few of the comments that our pupils made about the example we gave and consider how to develop some of the strategies they mentioned.

Pupil strategy  This strategy refers to familiarity with the linguistic context and with a knowledge of what certain texts look like.

Teaching strategy

In order to build on this, it may, for example, help pupils to have pointed out to them such basic information as:

- proper nouns will have capital letters;
- sentences end with full stops;
- punctuation such as exclamation and question marks aids comprehension;
- many words look similar in both languages;
- knowledge of print convention can help understanding (the layout of the page, the particular type of text, e.g. a recipe, a newspaper article).

Pupil strategy

> ☑ The photo was of a crash and there was 'accident' in the headline, so I knew what sort of words to look out for.

This strategy refers to prediction. It may then be helpful for pupils to engage in activities that ask them to predict the type of vocabulary they could expect to find in a particular context.

Teaching strategy

Before reading the article above, pupils were given the context ('Ein Profil von Liz', *Europafan*). This enabled them to predict, with or without the intervention of the teacher, that the article might include details of:

- age;
- where she lives;
- possible countries she knows;
- languages spoken;
- her opinions;
- future plans.

A follow-on activity could then be to predict the actual language that might feature in the article.

Pupil strategy

> ☑ I worked out the meaning of the words from looking them up.

This strategy underlines the importance of being able to use reference materials such as glossaries and dictionaries.

Teaching strategy

Alphabetical order

With some pupils a necessary starting point may be the concept of alphabetical order. Teachers may begin with activities such as:

- pupils get into alphabetical order;
- sort words on cards into alphabetical order;
- find the first word in the dictionary beginning with a stated combination of letters;
- find in the dictionary the next or previous word in a sequence.

How the dictionary is organised

While these activities will help with familiarisation with the organisation of a dictionary, activities more specific to finding and checking meaning might include:

- matching words with pictures, using the dictionary to check meaning;
- choosing a correct definition from a choice of three;
- finding the meaning of a word in the shortest possible time;
- searching for the next or previous 'header word'.

Finding meaning

- Find two or three different dictionaries' translation of the same word.
- Give three definitions of a word and ask pupils to search for the correct one.
- Give a list of compound words and ask pupils to break down each of them, looking up as many different parts as possible in the dictionary, e.g. *Frühstücksfernsehen*.
- Give a list of words and ask pupils to check in the dictionary which are in the same category, e.g. *collège, école, écurie, lycée*.
- Give pupils a list of words from which they have to look for the false friends, e.g. *baskets, cinéma, pull, radio*.

Checking for accuracy

- Find all the feminine nouns on a particular page of the dictionary.
- Find the incorrect spelling in a given list of words.
- Find the past participles of a given list of verbs.
- Find which words in a given list are different forms of the same word, e.g. *Schüler, Schulen, Schülers, Schülern*.

Pupil strategy

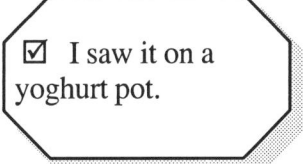

This refers to the fact that pupils are open to influences outside the classroom and that the teacher is not the only source of language.

Teaching strategy

It is useful to remind pupils of other areas where they may come across the language in a clear context which will support their comprehension: labels on food and clothes, posters, bilingual public notices, satellite television, radio, foreign language assistant, visitors from the country, British TV advertisements.

Pupil strategy

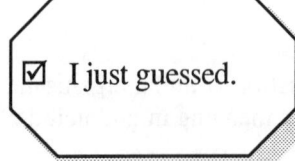

> ☑ I just guessed.

Teaching strategy

While not wanting to encourage wild guessing, guessing within a clear context should be encouraged. The teacher could blank out words in target language headlines and ask pupils to guess the missing word, possibly using a dictionary.

We would not wish to suggest that a teacher should spend a whole lesson on any one of these activities but rather that they are viewed as short, quick events which may take place every lesson, once a week or once every other week. What is important is that pupils become accustomed to using reference materials on a regular basis.

READING THE WHOLE TEXT

Though it is very valuable to encourage pupils to recognise individual lexical items, they must also realise from early on that the whole text is more than the sum of the individual parts that make it up. Pupils need to avoid the view that a text is an agglomeration of individual words each requiring decoding. When reading in one's mother tongue we consider not just the meaning of individual words, but the whole text in its entirety, be it a quarter page, a half page or a whole book. Encouraging pupils beginning to read in another language to look at the overall structure and message of a text rather than individual items of information contained in single words is important. But it is necessary to develop this alongside vocabulary building activities such as those we have referred to.

Some approaches to whole texts

Jigsaw texts

Rather than presenting pupils with the complete text immediately, they are given a version in which the main sections or paragraphs have been jumbled. Their task is to reorder and compare their finished version with the original. This might be done using IT.

Matching headlines to text

Pupils are presented with a series of short texts from which the titles or headlines have been removed. These are given in a separate list and pupils have to match the headlines and texts.

Source: *Mistral 2* (OUP, 1992)

*Weighing up **all** the evidence*

Pupils are presented with a text in which the writer makes both positive and negative statements. They have to decide, on balance, the writer's overall attitude to the subject, e.g. a French visitor compares facilities in a particular town in England and her home town in France. Pupils have to decide, by reading the whole text, which place the writer prefers.

Looking for themes

The teacher provides category headings and the pupils have to find and note all the relevant words in the text, e.g. weather, time, place, movement, feelings, colours.

Typographical layout

To remind pupils how helpful layout can be, they could be given examples of 'raw' texts where all layout has been removed. The first activity could be to identify which, for example, is the letter, the recipe, the newspaper article, the poster. With the aid of IT this could then be extended into an exercise where they have to recreate the original layout.

2. Making the most of available texts

Teachers intent on developing pupils' reading skills come up against a recurring problem: foreign language coursebooks, especially for the early years of language learning, provide relatively few extended texts for reading. There will be an attractive range of posters, brochures and other visually appealing realia but often few texts of any substantial length. And yet, even if the ultimate goal is a classroom of pupils working independently, choosing what they want to read for themselves, the teacher will need to develop the pupils' reading skills with explicit work in class that includes dealing with substantial texts. It may be possible to develop some material specifically for this but equally it is necessary to exploit available coursebooks. The examples that follow show how a range of strategies can be developed with material that may at first glance appear to have limited potential.

GETTING STARTED - GIVING PUPILS CONFIDENCE

Source: Zickzack Book 1
(Arnold-Wheaton, 1987)

This text illustrates some of the problems that face teachers and learners. It is the first of any substantial length that learners encounter, after about a year of language learning. The first problem is its overall size. Pupils may instinctively feel it is going to be difficult because of its length, and this may affect their confidence in dealing with it. Although the text has been subdivided into small sections of similar type of language (information about a person, age, job and opinions about the town) this could possibly act as a deterrent as much as an aid, if they realise they have to plough through twelve paragraphs of similar types of information.

The following tasks were designed to encourage pupils of all levels of attainment to approach the text positively.

Initial skimming

	Alter	Mann	Frau	Name	Nationalität *siehe Seite 3!*	Beruf	+ ? (auf englisch)
3	14	√		Ali T.	T	Schüler (?)	
4	15		√	Ellen.M.	D	Schülerin ~~Schüler~~	
9	16		√	Laura.M.	I	Schülerin	father has pizza parlour.
8	19	√		Volker.S.	D	Soldat	
10	21		√	Heide.L.	D	studiere	Fußgängerzone
7	23	√		Jochen.B.	D	Poilzist	Footballfan
12	34	√		Gerd.B.	D	Busfahrer	
11	37	√		Martin.F.	D	Lehrer	
5	38	√		Ian.G.	GB	Soldat	house
2	42	√		Kurt.Z.	D	Verkäufer	

The types of information that the pupils are to look for are arranged at the top of the grid - age, sex, name, nationality, occupation and 'any other information'. The age column has been partly filled in and the first task is to complete all the ages in ascending order. This is not a linguistic task as all the numbers are given in numerals, but it allows the reader to skim the whole text with some confidence and with a purpose in mind, sorting them into the right order. Rather than looking at specific details the learner reads the whole body of the text.

Choosing what to look for, and how

Once this has been completed, the only rule for working through the other categories is that pupils should work vertically, looking for a specific type of information through the whole text. This allows the pupil to build up confidence for the text as a whole and to focus on a particular type of information. The other categories have not been arranged particularly in increasing order of difficulty and it is not implied that the pupils should simply work from left to right. Rather, before starting, the pupil needs to decide the order in which they will choose to deal with the columns. This reflection on why they might find some columns easier than others - *I'm going to start with names because they will have capital letters, I'm going to start with sex because the drawings usually help me although I may have to check some names* - may need to be instigated by the teacher, training the pupils to consider how they can look for a certain type of information.

The bottom line expectation for pupils of all levels of attainment is that they will have completed the vertical searches that they planned to do and that some will have completed most of the searches. Peripheral vision will of course mean that the pupils will notice pieces of information from other searches that they are not involved with (they could be challenged not to note this until they start that search), thus building up memory and awareness of overall structure.

Keeping in the target language

As the base aim is to build confidence in how to look at whole texts, most of the searches are not particularly linguistically challenging. *Beruf* (job) may raise a problem as, if we are intent in keeping the task in the target language, how can we be certain that the language has really been understood? The example shown may not provide conclusive evidence that the pupil knew what *Verkäufer* or *Lehrer* meant, and the wrong part of the verb has been noted for *studiere - am studying* rather than *is studying*. It does, however, show that the correct word has been selected - the pupil is at least half way there and is developing the skill of identifying key words that matter. The teacher might want to check some meanings with pupils on an individual basis.

Doing a bit extra

The column on the right, '+? (*auf englisch*)', is more open-ended for the pupils to note what they have understood, rather than what the teacher wants them to understand. It is also important in helping the pupil understand that they have never really finished with a text, there is always something more they can get out of it. The occasional use of English here should not be seen as problematic and if the information is taken up or developed orally by the teacher it should be easy to use the information in the target language.

More intensive work

Another stage, if it is felt appropriate, could then be to look at one part of the text in more detail. This might include mixed-skills tasks such as devising an interview with the person or writing extra imagined information about them. Tasks that focus on the syntax in a manageable way could include gap filling, unjumbling sentences, adding extra words to enhance the meaning - *Die haben* sehr *gutes Bier* and removing words without affecting the overall meaning - *Da gibt es (schöne) Kneipen*.

TEXTS ARE NOT ANSWERS TO QUESTIONS

An unfortunate effect of many 'questions on texts' exercises can be that pupils see the text purely as a repository of answers to be extracted. Some pupils, when given a reader, will start by going to the tasks at the back and 'reading' the book in terms of answering the tasks.

This text is an example of 'tourist brochurese', short and in fairly controlled language which does nonetheless lend itself to a variety of approaches outlined below.

Si vous avez faim ou soif en France, allez dans un café. Les cafés en France sont ouverts toute la journée à partir de huit heures le matin ou plus tôt, jusqu'à minuit, ou plus tard.

Les Français vont au café pour s'amuser, pour rencontrer des amis, pour jouer aux cartes, aux dominos ou au babyfoot. Tout le monde—enfants et adultes—peut aller au café.

Souvent, il y a des tables et des chaises sur le trottoir, devant le café—sur la terrasse. Quand il fait beau, il est très agréable de s'asseoir à la terrasse et de prendre un verre.

On peut acheter toutes sortes de boissons dans un café en France—des boissons chaudes comme, par exemple, du café, du thé, du chocolat; des boissons froides comme de la limonade, du lait ou un jus de fruit; et des boissons alcoolisées comme de la bière ou du vin.

Et si vous avez faim, on vend des sandwichs et des casse-croûtes dans beaucoup de cafés.

Source: Tricolore 2, Pupil's book (E J Arnold, 1981)

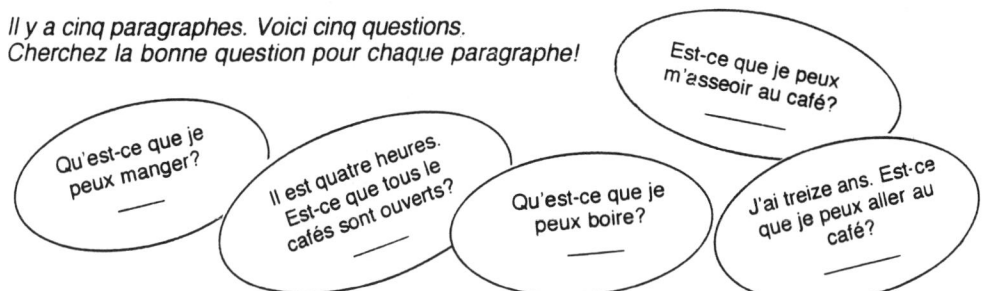

Il y a cinq paragraphes. Voici cinq questions. Cherchez la bonne question pour chaque paragraphe!

Lisez les phrases suivantes Qu'est-ce qui est vrai? Qu'est-ce qui est faux? Ou est-ce que c'est impossible à dire?

	C'est vrai	C'est faux!	Impossible à dire.
Les cafés sont encore ouverts à 1.00 du matin.			
Il y a beaucoup à faire au café.			
Les enfants sont interdits aux cafés français.			
On ne va pas au café quand il fait beau.			
On vend des boissons non-alcoolisées.			
Tous les cafés ont un grand menu.			
Il n'y a pas de différences entre les cafés français et les pubs anglais.			
Chaque café a une terrasse.			
On peut manger des snacks au café.			
On peut jouer aux échecs au café.			

Vous avez fini?
Fais une flash-publicité pour la radio. Encouragez les français à aller au café!(maximum 30 secondes)

Headlines

The initial task should again be to grasp the whole text, done here by matching headlines to paragraphs. In this case the headlines are questions that each paragraph gives an answer to.

True or false?

The second task which requires more detailed understanding is a standard true or false exercise but with a difference. The addition of the third column *'impossible à dire'* - *'you can't tell'* helps avoid the problem of random guessing but also encourages the pupil to adopt a different attitude to the text: that it may not provide answers to the questions asked. This is an approach to written evidence that they will be familiar with in other curriculum areas, such as when dealing with historical documents. When pupils tackled this activity they were divided as to whether there was enough evidence to prove that *every café has a terrace*. Both were accepted and the discussion that took place in simple French was more useful than having a definitive answer.

An extension task

Suitable extension tasks might be to write the script for, and record, a thirty second advertisement encouraging people to go to the café.

Setting up the task

Presenting the task in the target language can create a problem given the amount of French on the worksheet. Checking that pupils understand the true or false statements can be done collectively - *you have three minutes with a partner to underline all the words you know and decide which of these statements you understand - you don't have to start at the beginning,* followed by a class brainstorming and then targeting the sentences that nobody knew. This checking may be appropriate in English or by mimes. The preparation for this task effectively becomes another reading task, and it perhaps may be felt that it takes up a disproportionate amount of time. Nonetheless, the activity is valid in itself, it can include other skills such as speaking, and has already prepared the pupils for some of the language and ideas they are going to encounter in the text.

USING LONGER TEXTS

The subject of the following example, designed for middle and high attaining pupils preparing for public examination, may seem rather dry and the layout, with the questions in English at the bottom of the text, may tempt pupils merely to look for those answers. The lesson described was intended to cover the topic area of school in a way that challenged the predictability that can beset exam preparation.

Background reading: Unterschiede zwischen deutschen und englischen Schulen

Das deutsche Schulsystem ist ganz anders als das englische. Alle jungen Schüler im Alter von sechs bis zehn Jahren besuchen die gleiche Schule (Grundschule), aber für die älteren gibt es drei verschiedene Schularten: die Hauptschule (zehn bis fünfzehn Jahre), die Realschule (zehn bis sechzehn Jahre) und das Gymnasium (zehn bis neunzehn Jahre). In einigen Bundesländern gibt es auch Gesamtschulen.

Ein Schuljahr hat zwei Halbjahre; am Ende des Schuljahres (im Sommer) bekommen die Schüler ein Zeugnis. Wenn ein Schüler sehr schlecht in der Schule war, bleibt er sitzen. Er muß dann ein Jahr wiederholen!

Eine Realschule.

Die Schulferien sind so lang wie in Großbritannien aber die deutschen Schulen haben keinen Nachmittagsunterricht! Dafür ist aber auch am Samstag bis zwölf Uhr Schule. Gewöhnlich beginnt der Schultag schon um acht Uhr morgens! Eine Schulstunde dauert 45 Minuten; danach kommt eine kurze Pause. Es gibt sechs Schulstunden am Tag. Die Schüler bleiben zum Mittagessen nicht in der Schule, denn schon ungefähr um Viertel nach eins ist die Schule zu Ende, so daß sie zu Hause essen können. Für die Pausen nehmen sie oft belegte Brote und Obst mit, und in vielen Schulen können sie Milch und Süßigkeiten kaufen.

Ein Gymnasium.

Wenn eine Klasse nicht alle sechs Stunden Unterricht hat, dürfen die Schüler später zur Schule kommen oder früher wieder gehen. Nur manchmal müssen die älteren Schüler auch nachmittags zur Schule.

Am Nachmittag oder abends müssen die Schüler meistens eine bis zwei Stunden lang Hausaufgaben machen. Trotzdem aber haben sie jeden Tag Zeit für ihre Hobbies.

An sehr heißen Sommertagen gibt es hitzefrei. Dann dürfen alle Schüler und Lehrer nach Hause gehen! Aber auch im Winter muß die Schule manchmal ausfallen, wenn so viel Schnee liegt, daß die Schüler nicht mit dem Fahrrad oder dem Bus zur Schule fahren können.

In der Physikstunde.

1 What do we learn about different types of schools in Germany?
2 What do we learn about the school year and about reports?
3 What happens to pupils whose progress is bad?
4 What details are given about school hours and the school day?
5 What do German pupils do about meals on school days?
6 What freedom do German pupils enjoy with respect to going to and from school?
7 What is said about after-school activities?
8 What two reasons are given for school closing?

Source: Fertig! (OUP, 1984)

Whole class warm-up activities

Even with more experienced language learners it can be useful to build up a feeling for the whole text before looking at it in detail. The two first tasks for the pupils are designed to be quick skimming, confidence boosting exercises.

1. Scanning - word counts

As a warm-up, pupils here were asked to find as many words as possible that contained the keyword of the passage - *Schul(e)*. They were encouraged not necessarily to start at the top, and it was done quickly in pairs with an element of challenge - *'you have two minutes to find as many Schul(e) words as possible'*. These were then brainstormed by the whole class. Useful issues arose (such as whether *Schüler* is an acceptable word, and what are different forms of the same word, e.g. *Schule/Schulen*).

2. Scanning - word types

Done briskly, a second skimming exercise was used which was linguistically more demanding. Again in pairs, the pupils were asked to find as many words as possible related to time in any forms of speech - *Minute, oft, Jahr* - and then to arrange them chronologically from the shortest to the longest. This demanded more thought, but again pupils worked effectively in pairs, and with a time limit, followed by a class brainstorming.

Not all texts may be as yielding as this, but it is often possible to find certain types of recurring language. (A useful initial scanning activity, particularly with French texts, can be to find the cognates and to decide if the meaning is the same in both languages (*faux-amis*).) A final whole text activity was matching headlines to paragraphs, again done in pairs. The teacher may not want to do all of these activities but there is usefulness in having a *variety* of quick whole text tasks which give the reader an overall feel for the text in a non-threatening way (pair-work and pooled information).

3. Headlines for the paragraphs

To give pupils an overall awareness of the content of the passage, headlines were given each to be attached to a paragraph.

Intensive reading

After these graded warming up activities, designed to boost the pupil's awareness of the text as a whole, we wanted to look at the text in more detail.

4. 'The bleeding chunk' - identifying paraphrases

Der dritte Absatz (Die Schulferien...) besteht aus 6 Sätzen. Welche Sätze hier unten passen zu welchen Sätzen im Text?

a: Eine Stunde ist nur fünfundvierzig Minuten lang.

> b: Schüler essen und trinken zwischen den Schulstunden.
>
> c: Es gibt keine Kantine in den meisten deutschen Schulen.
>
> d: Die Schule ist gegen 13 Uhr aus.
>
> e: Man hat sechs Stunden jeden Tag.
>
> f: Deutsche Schüler haben sechs Tage Schule in der Woche.

The length and density of the text precluded starting at the beginning and working our way to the end. We chose the most demanding paragraph as a starting point, a 'bleeding chunk', irrespective of its place in the overall structure of the text.

Rather than do a direct translation, the pupils were given a paraphrase matching exercise for each of the six sentences in the paragraph, to be done in pairs. The teacher can grade this task to suit the level of attainment of the pupils by the number of clues given in the paraphrases. In this instance the pupils had to read each statement carefully as there appeared to be more than one possible answer.

5. *Group work 1 - intensive* précis/translation

It would have been unrealistic and repetitive to have done the rest of the text in this way. Instead, the class was broken up into five groups of six pupils each to specialise on one of the paragraphs. The task they had was straightforward - to come up with an agreed *précis* in English covering the main points of the paragraph in half the number of words in the original. To make certain this was a group activity, all members of the group had to agree on and record the same points. This was the most demanding of all the tasks and pupils were encouraged to use reference materials and query moot points with the teacher if need be. The task could have differed - it could equally have been a straight translation or even possibly a *précis* in German - for variety, and dependent on the level of attainment of the pupils.

6. *Group work 2 - reporting back*

The second group task involved self-selected groups containing a representative from each of the above groups. Each representative had to report on their paragraph. It was suggested that the others make very brief notes on what they heard, but they were not encouraged to attempt verbatim accounts of everything they were told.

7. *Follow-up activities*

The pupils now had built up, by various methods, a detailed awareness of the whole text within a 55-minute lesson. The follow-up activities included answering the GCSE type questions in English at the bottom of the text, which was done quickly and without problems, and a written task in German, comparing the German and English school system, as the text provided a good variety of appropriate vocabulary.

A generic method

This method of dealing with longer texts - a combination of overview and intensive, and whole class and group work can also work effectively with groups of different levels of attainment. It has been used successfully with GCSE Basic candidates working with letters developing their reading and writing skills.

The same approach can also be an effective way into literary texts for more advanced students. Rather than working through a book initially in a linear, possibly rather laborious manner, a combination of different methods of working can be usefully applied, scanning the books for e.g. characters and settings, selecting attractive 'bleeding chunks' for intensive work, irrespective of where they come in the sequence of events. The final activity, akin to answering the questions in English in the example above, would be to ask the pupils, with all the experience of the text that they have built up, to read the whole text on their own, independently, as they might when reading in English.

DEVELOPING NARRATIVE AWARENESS

The examples so far have concentrated on factual texts. When considering fiction another aspect that needs to be considered is awareness of a story line, how to follow a narrative.

A good starting point is cartoon stories, as they appear in many coursebooks, are of manageable length and provide plenty of visual clues. A problem can be that the pupils are naturally drawn to the punchline without looking closely at the text, and once this has been done there may not be the necessary motivation to go back and work more intensively on the language content. These two examples suggest how to motivate pupils to want to read the text closely.

Writing before reading

Before the pupils see the completed text they are given a blanked out version.

Rather than simply giving the pupils jumbled up speech balloons to copy, they are asked to fill them in with their own language but arriving at the same punchline. The obvious danger with this is that pupils will be adventurous and will try to write more than they are capable of. To avoid this, they are told to use the basic transactional language (*How do I get to...*, *It's far...*, *Take the bus...*, etc) and then to flesh it out only with other phrases in the foreign language that they already know. This provides a good variety of language, a feeling that each story is different and that in a limited, if highly structured way, pupils are able to display some creativity.

Having completed their stories the pupils read the original story in the book, reading each caption carefully to see how far it resembled their own version. Sometimes theirs is a better version than the one in the book!

Wo ist das Hallenbad?

Wo ist das Hallenbad?

Source: Zickzack Book 1 (Arnold-Wheaton, 1987)

Organising the story line

An alternative method is to give pupils a jumbled paraphrased version before seeing the original story. The paraphrases can be in very simple language.

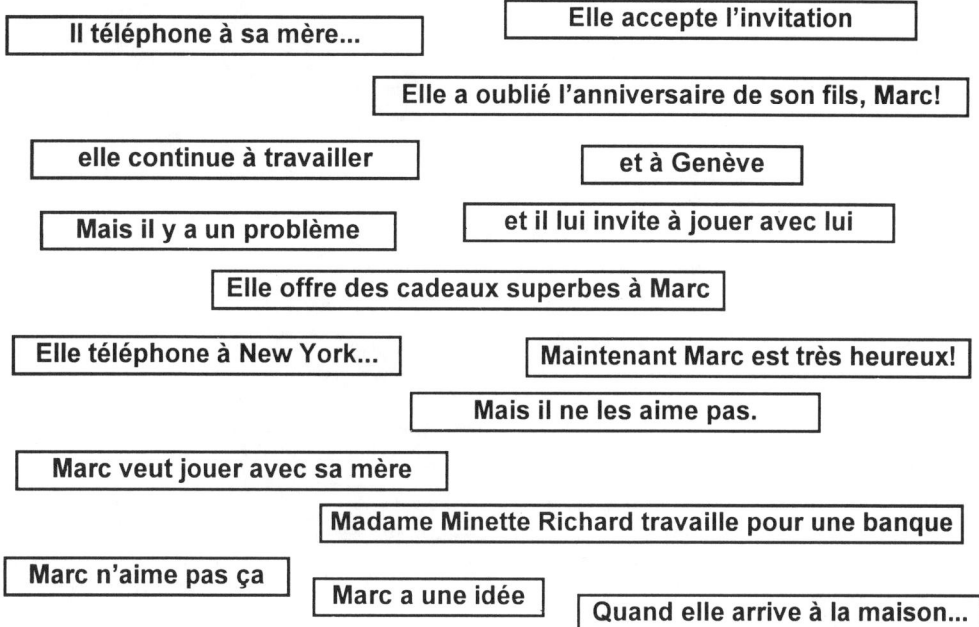

Most pupils will benefit from some guidance in dealing with these phrases.

- How many different people are there in the story?
- Can they make a column of sentences (in any order) for each person?
  (This will help them relate pronouns to proper names - *il/Marc, elle/Madam Minette*)
- Some sentences are incomplete - can they join up any parts?
- Can they match up any pairs of sentences?
- What do they think the first/last sentence of the story might be?

At this point the pupils could be encouraged, in pairs, to decide on their overall order for their version of the story. Once these have been discussed with at least one other pair the original version in the book could be examined. Once again the way the pupils read this version will be different from reading in their own language. They will be comparing this version with their own and looking for clues that substantiate the paraphrases, both of which require close attention to the text. They have a reason for reading.

Source: Etoiles 1 (BBC/Longman, 1992)

Exploiting pre-knowledge

Readers come to stories with all sorts of expectations of what is possible in terms of types of character, settings, possible storylines. One particularly useful piece of information for language learners for example is that, if they already know the story in their own language, they will be aware of the overall structure and maybe even some key words.

The original starting point for the following activity was material written by foreign language assistants. They had been asked to write short versions of different fairy stories. They produced a number of different versions of the same story.

To prepare the pupils they were given a sheet containing jumbled key words and titles from three different stories. They had to decide what words fitted with which story (doing as much as they could initially without, and then with, the aid of dictionaries).

Faites trois listes des mots clés!

- cent ans plus tard
- des chaussures de verre
- à minuit
- une marraine fée
- les sept nains
- elle vivait avec son père
- un carrosse
- **Cendrillon**
- un château
- sa peau si blanche
- une pomme empoisonnée
- une méchante fée
- **La Belle au Bois Dormant**
- **Blanche Neige**
- se piqua
- sa belle mère

Having agreed as a class on the sorting of these three categories the next task was to arrange these words in the order in which they would occur in the story. The pupils then had to add four more key words of their own that they thought might appear.

As there were a minimum of five versions of each complete story, pupils were able to read at least some of them and make comparisons between them and with their own original predictions.

Another more open-ended activity is to brainstorm with pupils the types of words they might encounter in the text. Versions written by the assistants have also provided a useful stepping stone to 'real French' versions, such as the *Contes* by Perrault.

No pre-knowledge?

Apart from this specific example of fairy tales, pre-knowledge of most stories will be unlikely but a simple checklist completed in advance could encourage pupils to think about how a story might develop:

> *Avant de lire* Agent secret numéro neuf *fais tes prédictions!*
> - *L'agent est un homme ou une femme?*
> - *L'agent cherche des bijoux/une femme/un scientifique?*
> - *L'agent va en avion/en voiture?*
> - *L'agent n'a pas de succès. Oui ou non?*

Pre-knowledge of factual texts may sometimes exist, if partially and inaccurately. Before reading a text about e.g. the differences between schools in France and England, pupils could look at this list and make their own decisions about which apply to which country. They then compare their predictions with what the writer feels, deciding at the same time whether they disagree with anything the writer has said.

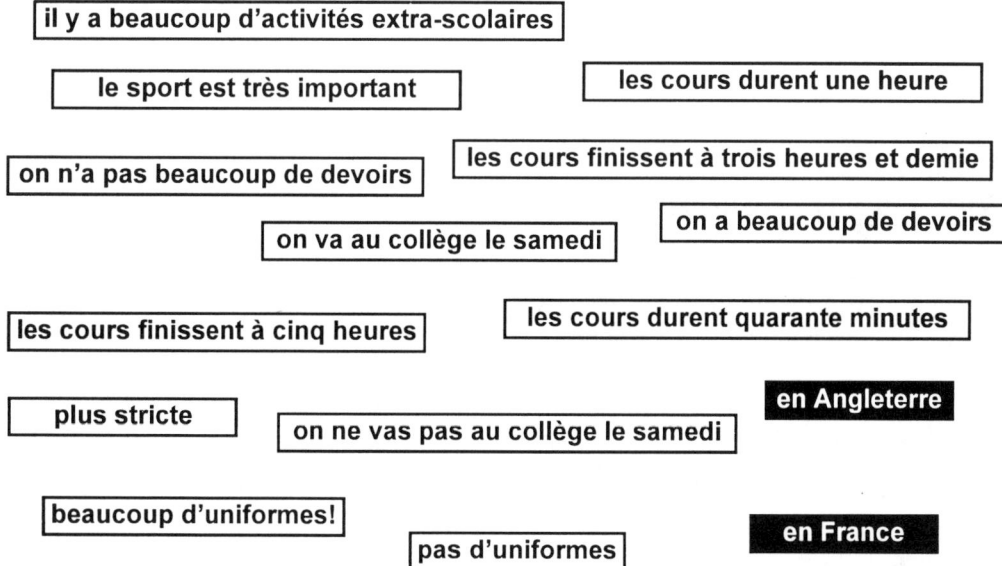

1) En France, à l'école, les élèves étudient toutes les matières comme base générale. (Français, Histoire, Géographie, Mathématiques, Sciences physiques/naturelles, éducation physique, Anglais)

2) En France, les élèves ont plus d'heures de cours dans la journée, environ 7 heures.

3) En France, il y a deux récréations. Une le matin vers 10h 15mn, une l'après-midi vers 15h.

4) En France, les élèves ne portent pas d'uniforme.

5) En France, les élèves ont des feuilles de papier à carreaux.

6) En France, les notes sont importantes pour le passage dans la classe supérieure.

7) En France, si un élève ne travaille pas bien, il redouble sa classe.

8) En France, l'école finit à 5:00 pm.

9) En France, les élèves étudient la grammaire anglaise ou allemande ou espagnole.

10) En France, les élèves amènent et ramènent leurs livres... leurs cartables sont lourds...

WHY WAS A TEXT WRITTEN?

The examples of texts looked at so far cover a range of factual and imaginative writing. Although it may seem too sophisticated a discussion to have in the foreign language, it is also worth asking pupils to consider *why* the text was actually written.

Having done a variety of extensive and intensive exercises on a tourist brochure with a Year 10 group, a final task was to consider *who* would have written it and *how* this would have affected the way it was written. Having established that the writer of a tourist brochure would want visitors to come to the area described, pupils then managed to identify some of the ways in which the writer was trying to achieve this. Use of superlative adjectives, phrases like *weltberühmt* (world famous), positive references to the weather were all identified.

Although some other texts may be less yielding to this approach, they have all nevertheless been written for a purpose, even if only to convey information. The writer of the example *Schulen in Deutschland* wanted to give English readers information about German schools - consequently there are a large number of facts included for English readers. The writer of *Madame Minette* wants to highlight Marc's problems with his mother - thus there are many contrasts made between what his mother does and what he wants.

3. Developing a policy for independent reading

The concern to encourage pupils to read independently is not new. Indeed, the presence of dusty readers from the sixties in stock cupboards throughout the country bears witness to this. As William Rowlinson points out:

> *Ideas... have a habit of coming into and going out of fashion. What is taught and how it is taught is a product of these ideas, as well as of the conditions in which it is to be taught... many, perhaps most, new approaches are rediscoveries of old methods neglected and left in the shade, now re-illuminated by the light of social need.*
> (Rowlinson, 1985)

Independent reading is a case in point. Encouraged by the introduction of the National Curriculum, MFL departments are keen for their pupils to develop their independence as linguists and reading plays a central part in this development, as Grenfell suggests:

> *It is, after all, the least inhibiting of the four skills; the most comfortable to work with. Pupils can work at their own pace, reading, re-reading, checking and responding with their own thought patterns. At the very least this frees lessons from over-domination by the teacher.*
> (Grenfell, 1992)

There has been a growth in demand for suitable texts with the result that a wide selection of extended texts is being published to cater for the adolescent reader.

In departments where independent reading has become a priority, it is common to find that a reading policy has been drawn up to ensure that all pupils have equal access to books and equal opportunity to read independently. The provision differs from school to school. Some provide a mobile bank of different texts for pupils and staff to use when needed, while others have set up systematised reading schemes situated in the school library or in a dedicated languages room.

SETTING UP AN INDEPENDENT READING SCHEME

There are practical issues beyond the availability and provision of suitable texts which need to be addressed if a department is considering setting up a reading scheme. Issues range from how structured the scheme should be to how much monitoring will be required by the teacher, to the link between independent reading and other classroom activities, and to the need for a programme of developing reading skills in general. Other issues which need to be discussed are:

- the amount of teacher involvement required during an independent reading lesson;
- access to dictionaries;
- whether there should be multiple copies of popular books available;
- where the books should be housed (in the school library or in a classroom or on a trolley);
- whether books should be on loan;
- whether there should be scheduled reading periods;
- whether there might be a reading club;
- whether pupils should be set targets (e.g. to read at least one book and one magazine per term);
- what titles should be provided (the balance between fiction and non-fiction);
- whether pupils should complete comprehension exercises after finishing a book;
- whether pupils should keep a record of what they have read;
- the storage system.

Once these issues have been resolved, then a department might move towards drawing up a reading policy. Below are examples of two schools' policy documents, one from Avon and the other from Cambridgeshire.

The Grange School, Avon

Reading policy

Reading is an authentic activity and an essential part of the language learning process. It reinforces structure and vocabulary already used as well as introducing pupils to language not previously encountered. From the beginning, reading should be seen as a pleasurable and useful activity which has purposes other than purely linguistic ones. In order to encourage this attitude, reading activities should require pupils to carry out tasks (e.g. follow recipes, instructions for making things), use problem solving skills (e.g. games, logic puzzles), link reading to other skills (i.e. multi-skill activities), give pupils the opportunity to exercise choice and read for pleasure, give pupils the opportunity to respond creatively to what they have read.

All of the above are an integral part of language learning. Reading for pleasure, in particular, is a timetabled part of lessons in the faculty and takes place in the library. The languages section contains a selection of graded reading material, authentic and non-authentic, books and magazines, fiction and non-fiction. Lessons take place in the library as follows:

Year 7: 1 lesson every 2/3 weeks from Christmas.
Year 8: 1 lesson every 2 weeks.
Year 9: 1 lesson every week for single linguists, and every so often for double linguists as judged to be appropriate by the teacher.
Years 10 and 11: 1 lesson every 2/3 weeks, if time allows.

In these lessons pupils choose the books/magazines they wish to read and fill in a reading diary showing their progress, enjoyment and response. The behaviour expected of pupils is that appropriate to the library context; pupils must read in silence. Books must be replaced neatly and in the correct place.

Reading diaries are to be regularly checked and marked by teachers, in order to ensure that the necessary amount is being done and that diaries are being filled in correctly. Teachers should also encourage pupils to write increasingly complex summaries and comments. In order to encourage a creative response from pupils on occasions (e.g. once a term) the format, and if appropriate the location, of the reading lesson should be changed to allow for activities of a more productive nature based on the books read (e.g. making a radio play).

Cottenham Village College

Independent Reading Programme: Years 7 - 11

The National Curriculum Draft Proposals state in the Programme of Study Part 1 that *'pupils should be given opportunities to:*

2e ... read for personal interest or enjoyment
2i ... develop dictionary skills
2k ... read ... texts of different types and of varying lengths
3l ... work with authentic materials
and
> *deal with increasingly complex texts...*
> *show increasing independence in language learning'*

The Independent Reading Programme is designed to help achieve all of these aims, for pupils of all abilities, and at all stages of language learning. The department has invested in a variety of reading material: authentic 'real books', sets of readers for language learners and language magazines. There is at present a lot more material available for French than for German, particularly in structured reading schemes, but it is hoped that more German material will be added when it becomes available.

The two main elements are:

The reading box
For each year there is a **reading box** which will contain a variety of material appropriate to the year. For KS3 this will have more emphasis on structured readers and short reading cards and KS4 boxes will have predominantly more 'real books' (although there will be an overlap both ways). This will be supplemented by some duplicate copies and other material in the school library.

The reading period
In order to raise the profile of such reading, and to establish good habits, it is suggested that each class should have a regular, timetabled **30-minute reading session** once a fortnight. Teachers will need to book the **reading box** and a set of dictionaries for this half period.

Some points to consider...

Choice of books
Each box is structured with the ability of the pupils in mind. Teachers will however need to offer some guidance to pupils so that they do not make unrealistic choices and become disillusioned. Where there are graded readers this can be done easily

but it would be wrong however not to allow even weaker pupils on occasions to dip into more difficult books to whet their appetites. It will not be possible to borrow books from the box but it is envisaged that the school library will also stock a selection of the titles that can be borrowed in the usual way. Remember also that pupils' recommendations to each other can be very effective and a pupils' bulletin board/OHT of what they have enjoyed is worth considering.

The teacher's role
During reading periods, reading should be the main activity, i.e. the material should not be treated as 'something for the rest to do while the teacher does x, y or z with individual pupils' and it would obviously help if the teacher was able to set an example as well by reading for at least some of the time. The teacher may also want on occasions to read with individual pupils and should also monitor progress, i.e. 'Before you go on to a new book you must come to me' and perhaps have a short conversation '*C'était bon? Non? Pourquoi?*'

Reading skills
It is possible that we make too many assumptions about the pupils' ability to read books, even in their own language. Problems that pupils may encounter when reading in another language could include an inability to concentrate on the amount of text, a lack of confidence that they can understand the main points of the story. As the aim of this programme is to encourage independence and enjoyment it is probably inappropriate to use such material overtly to teach reading skills. But it does mean that one of our aims in our classwork with class texts (from e.g. the textbook) must be to develop confidence and the pupils' ability to identify the main points of a narrative.

What does this mean? - **using reference material**
Only some of the material will contain word lists so it will be necessary for pupils to become familiar with the use of dictionaries. The *Developing dictionary skills* booklet by Cambridgeshire LEA provides a good variety of strategies for the teacher although this will have to be done separately from the reading period. Pupils also need to be reminded that there are other ways of discovering meaning - seeing if it looks like an English word, saying it, checking their own vocabulary lists, asking a neighbour or someone who has already read the book, possibly the assistant and even occasionally, as a last resort, the teacher. Teacher might want to establish a series of steps '*before you do this...*'.

Tasks and diaries
One of the aims must be to maintain a balance between reading and tasks on the reading as there can be a danger that pupils spend more time on the exercises than on reading. The tasks need to be kept in perspective although one task that pupils

should always do is to record a small number (4/5) of new words they have come across, with their meaning. It has been decided that it will not be necessary to have a formally printed reading diary in which pupils record their progress. Instead it will be felt adequate for them to record what and when they are reading, as well as new vocabulary, in a section of the notebooks they are also using for their listening work.

Other generic tasks that can easily be used with any material include:
- brief summaries;
- predictions about what will happen - how accurate were you?;
- make a cast list of all the people in the story;
- list of scenes/props needed for a film version;
- act out/record a very brief episode from a book, changing/adapting language.

Factual material
As well as stories there is a certain amount of factual material on the culture of the country, particularly in the library. In some ways, this is more difficult to exploit and pupils may want to dip into it on a more random basis. It may be more useful for KS4 pupils in linking with work on GCSE topics. Some generic activities that could work could be having a class collection of interesting facts culled from these sources and possible links with IT.

Book week
The reading period will not be appropriate for Year 7 pupils at the beginning of their course, but in October all Year 7 pupils will have the material presented to them in a high profile exercise involving displays, library work and presentations by older pupils of individual books.

Setting targets
The teacher will need to decide what are realistic targets for pupils but it may be worth stating that *'during the term/year everybody should have read at least x number of books'*. Pupils could also, after some time, be asked to select one book they have particularly enjoyed and to return to it and do some in-depth work on it. This could include devising activities for other readers, a poster recommending it, a short oral presentation to the class or to younger pupils (see above Year 7 - Book week) or a survey of what other people thought of it.

READING DIARIES

Where reading has become an important part of life in the languages classroom it is sometimes considered valuable for pupils to record what they have read in a reading diary. This provides the opportunity for pupils to reflect upon what they have read and to record their achievements. The diaries are usually records of pupils' independent reading and may take a very flexible format where the date is recorded together with a summary of what has been read; maybe forming part of an exercise book (as mentioned in the Cottenham Village College policy document above). Some schools have produced formatted reading diaries which guide pupils to reflect upon what they have read and to record their opinions. This is an example of the reading diary of a Year 9 pupil at Bassingbourn Village College in Cambridgeshire:

Titre / Titel	Karneval Krimi
Ecrit par / von	Sue Barratt
Commencé le / Begonnen am	den 8.3.93
Terminé le / Beendet am	den 8.3.93

Genre / Buchtyp	Abenteuer
Niveau / Schwierigkeit	Ziemlich schwierig
Avis / Meinung	Schlecht
Présentation / Ausgabe	lebendig
Recommandation / Empfehlung	vielleicht

Découvertes / Gefunden

français / Deustch	anglais / Englisch	dictionnaire / Wörterbuch
Polizei	Police	worked it out
Wieviel?	How much?	looked it up
Komm!	Come On!	worked it out

In this department, pupils have a timetabled reading lesson which takes place in the library where a large selection of French and German books are stored. Each pupil is issued with a diary and is expected to keep a record of what they read. The diary is a personal record and as such is not assessed by the teacher, but what is written in it can stimulate conversation between teacher and pupil since the teacher will occasionally take time to read through the diaries.

This is an example of a diary designed for Years 10 and 11 and allows for a more detailed response:

INFORMATIONS

Titre:
Auteur:
Je l'ai commencé le
Je l'ai terminé le

Un petit résumé en bref:

Je l'ai trouvé . . .

Ennuyeux	
Facile	
Mauvais	
Génial	
Intéressant	
Assez intéressant	
Très intéressant	
Difficile	
Superbe	
Touchant	
Lent	
Amusant	

Tragique	
Comique	
Romantique	
Réaliste	
Intellectuel	
Passionnant	
Sensationnel	

et aussi . . .

et aussi . . .

The diary as a dialogue

Another model of reading diary might take the form of a written dialogue between teacher and pupils where the pupil jots down impressions, interesting points and problems as they occur. The teacher then writes a reply in the diary. This form of diary may be more suitable for post-16 pupils tackling more sophisticated texts who will be studying in more depth than those lower down the school. One such system designed to develop critical reading skills is described by Grabrielle Cliff Hodges (Homerton College, Cambridge) in a pamphlet written by the 12-16 Committee of the National Association for the Teaching of English. Though the 'reading journal' described is for pupils of English, there are many messages for language teachers. Whether the journal is kept in the foreign language or English would be an issue to be discussed and decided by teacher and pupils together:

> *The value of using journals lies in pupils recording in some detail their initial encounters with texts rather than solely their final ideas and opinions. Pupils' journals thus include dated entries made at various stages before, during and after the reading of a text. The accumulated record of reading processes, developments, reflection and response will, in some cases, form the basis of more carefully shaped and considered coursework at a later stage. What it provides in the meantime though is a continuous record of reading of all kinds. The entries also form one side of a dialogue with the teacher about both the text and the processes of reading it... Although time is required on the part of the teacher for reading and responding to journal entries, it is also worth bearing in mind that pupils will neither want, nor will they need, to write one on every occasion they do some reading.*
> (Cliff Hodges, 1994)

Conclusion

Developing the reading habit amongst pupils, then, is not the sole domain of the English department. It is one of the responsibilities of all teachers. We, as language teachers, have a vast and rich resource in the literature and authentic texts of our target culture. But we need to develop our own interest in that culture by reading as widely as we can and by communicating that interest to our pupils. We ourselves need to be seen as enthusiastic and committed readers so that we become role models to our pupils. It may prove true that the reading habit can become contagious.

> *Reading is like an infectious disease; it is caught, not taught. (And you can't catch it from someone who hasn't got it.)*
> (Nuttall, 1982)

But we have learnt in the years since the first Pathfinder and since the re-emergence of interest in independent reading that motivating pupils to read and providing texts which they will enjoy does not fully equip them to develop their independence. We need also to think about explicitly teaching them strategies to use when meeting an unfamiliar text for the first time. In this way reading can become an exciting and enriching experience for pupils. We hope that this Pathfinder will go some way towards supporting you in your task.

References

Cliff Hodges G, *A rest from Shakespeare - developing independent reading in the secondary school* (National Association for the teaching of English - 12-16 Committee, 1994)

Giles Jones M, 'Reading - the poor relation - report of a modern languages in-service course', in *The British Journal of Language Teaching*, vol 26, no 2, Autumn 1988

Grenfell M, 'Reading and communication in the modern languages classroom - perspectives on reading', in the *Centre for Languages Education Working Papers*, no 2 (University of Southampton, 1992)

Nuttall C, *Teaching reading skills in a foreign language* (Heinemann Educational, 1982)

Rowlinson W, *Personally speaking - teaching languages for use - no 2* (Oxford University Press, 1985)